D1527646

Child Octopus

Child
Octopus

Edible
Adventures
in Hong Kong

MATTHEW AMSTER-BURTON

rootsandgrubs.com

Cover by CL Smith
Book design by Matthew Amster-Burton
All photographs © 2014 Matthew Amster-Burton except:
Photographs on pp. 25 and 39 © 2014 Iris Amster-Burton
Photograph on p. 28 taken by a woman at a viewpoint
Photograph on p. 69 © 2013 Nicolas Vollmer, CC-BY 2.0

ISBN 978-1-5025600-9-4

To my parents, Judy and Richard Amster

The Zip and Eat Series

Welcome to a new, occasional series about Asian food and travel. In each installment, a Seattle food writer (that's me!) and his daughter (that's Iris!) eat their way through a different city. A Zip and Eat Pocket Reader is the opposite of a guidebook. We're not experts. We just got here, and we're hungry.

Next up: Taipei. Coming in the future.

Hong Kong geography

Hong Kong is both a city and a region, made up of four parts:

Hong Kong Island is home to the skyline and Victoria

Peak. Just offshore from the mainland, Hong Kong Island is about the size of Manhattan, but its interior is mountainous. Hong Kong's rich—and there are a lot of them—live here. Hong Kongers often refer to the island as "Island-side," as opposed to "Kowloon-side." Well-known neighborhoods on the island include Central, Wan Chai, and Causeway Bay. The south side of the island is less developed and unreachable by subway (although that's about to change), and is home to the towns of Aberdeen and Stanley.

Kowloon is a small peninsula on the mainland, ending just across Victoria Harbor from Hong Kong island. The strait between them is slim enough that it's connected by two subway tunnels, three road tunnels, and a five-minute ferry ride, but no bridges. Compared to Hong Kong Island, Kowloon is smaller, more densely populated, and less rich. Well-known neighborhoods include Tsim Sha Tsui, Mong Kok, and Yau Ma Tei, where Iris and I stayed.

The New Territories extend north and east from Kowloon to the border of mainland China. They're huge, many times the size of Hong Kong Island and Kowloon put together, and a real mix: rural, parkland, towns and cities, and beaches.

The Outlying Islands, all 262 of them, include the huge Lantau (much larger than Hong Kong Island) and an array of smaller islands. Some are inhabited and are bedroom communities (Cheung Chau, Peng Chau, and Lamma); many are uninhabited. Have you noticed a large, unlabeled island on your tourist map of Hong Kong? It's probably Hei Ling Chau, the prison island and former leper colony.

Sea Star

The capitalists of Hong Kong have been terrific builders,
and have made of the great port, its hills and its harbors,
one of the most thrilling of all metropolitan prospects—
for my own tastes, the finest sight in Asia.
     —Jan Morris

Let's say you have one night in Hong Kong. You land at
Hong Kong International in the evening and take the Airport Express into town, watching the dotted blue progress
bar creep along, Windows 95–style, as the train carries you
from the airport to Tsing Yi to Kowloon to Hong Kong station.

You disembark and walk north on a long pedestrian
bridge, past the Apple Store seemingly suspended above
Connaught Road. Arriving at Central Pier, you tap your
Octopus card at Pier 7, and 30 cents is deducted from your
account. Moments later, a buzzer sounds, an electrified
gate swings open, and you make your way across the gangplank onto the lower deck of the Star Ferry and take a seat

in the back of the boat. Perhaps your vessel is the Shining Star, or the Solar Star, the Meridian Star or Silver Star.

With a diesel-fueled groan, the boat pushes off, and the skyline heaves into view. This is your welcome. Anyone who is not awed by their first ride on the Star Ferry has a stunted sense of wonder. The city is a lantern. There's the cocoon-shaped IFC Two, and I.M. Pei's Bank of China tower, but the individual buildings shimmer and dissolve and weave around each other as the ferry plies its five-minute course to Tsim Sha Tsui. Over on Kowloon-side, the International Commerce Center, Hong Kong's tallest building, stands alone, the entire structure wrapped in an animated light show featuring animals, flowers, messages in Chinese and English.

As the boat arrives at TST terminal, a uniformed employee tosses the end of a rope to his counterpart on the shore, who catches it with a hooked pole. Your guy on the boat wraps the rope around a mooring bitt, and the rope creaks as it pulls tight, lashing the boat to the dock.

The gangplank descends, and passengers stream off. Most are jaded, on their way to the next thing. You walk around the terminal, stop for a hot egg tart at Tai Cheong, and get back on board.

Going out for Chinese

I love Chinese food.

But who *doesn't* love Chinese food, right? I grew up eating it in Portland, Oregon, in the 1980s. This was in the pre-Portlandia days, when people in Portland wore normal-width pants and ate at restaurants like House of Louie and Fong Chong, places my family often went for dim sum. This was before food blogs, before online review sites, before most non-Chinese ten-year-olds had heard of dim sum. I remember eating sesame balls and pork buns, *har gow* shrimp dumplings and sticky rice wrapped in some kind of leaf. And I remember thinking, *Why can't we eat like this every day?*

I moved away from Portland right around the time it got cool, which has got to be a coincidence, right? My wife Laurie and I live in Seattle with our ten-year-old, Iris, who loves Chinese food as much as I ever did. I cook Chinese at home more than any other cuisine. Every weekend I ask Iris for her Pick of the Week, which I dutifully write down on the dinner calendar, and it's Chinese food at least three-quarters of the time. More, if you count Malaysian Chicken and Rice, which is really just a variation on Hainanese Chicken Rice, a dish from, yes, China.

So Iris and I decided to spend spring break in Hong Kong. Unlike mainland China, Hong Kong lets Americans in without a visa. We could spend a whole week indulging in assorted Picks of the Week—dim sum, seafood, noodles, street food—all in the same week. Maybe the same day. Flights from Seattle to Hong Kong are surprisingly inexpensive. The place is just sitting there on the other side of a big lake. Why wouldn't we go?

This wouldn't be our first Asian adventure. Iris and I went to Tokyo together for spring break when she was six. Everything went fine. She didn't get lost in Japan and adopted by the kindly owners of a sushi place, not that she would have minded. In fact, I'm designing a study abroad program based on this idea right now. Send your kid away for a semester; they come back and serve you *omakase*.

We've been back to Japan a couple of times, including one memorable July, when Laurie, Iris, and I lived in a tiny Tokyo apartment. I wrote a book about the experience called *Pretty Good Number One: An American Family Eats Tokyo,* exploring some of the lesser-known sides of Japanese food and culture.

After this, I figured, Hong Kong would be a snap. I eat and cook Chinese food all the time. I read books by Ken Hom and Fuchsia Dunlop in bed. Furthermore, English is widely spoken in Hong Kong, part of the legacy of colonialism. Iris and I could breeze in, live like locals for a week, eat our weight in Chinese food, and head home to tell America all about it.

Say, what's that smell? Oh yeah, it's hubris.

Hong Kong is a beautiful world city with great food. It's everything you love about Chinatown, writ large. And it's so goddamned frustrating. Nearly all of the frustration was my fault, for wanting Hong Kong to be something that it isn't—namely, Tokyo with Chinese food. Tokyo is orderly, effortlessly hospitable, obsessed with good manners. Hong Kong is none of the above. It's hard not to think of Hong Kong Island and Kowloon as Manhattan and Brooklyn, not just because of the geographical similarities but because both give off a seen-it-all, "you-talkin'-to-me?" big-city vibe.

In Hong Kong, Iris and I made new friends (some human, some feline), ate crispy rice from a clay pot, and sat in the front window of a double-decker bus. We also got seasick, lost, overtired, thirsty, and homesick. Moreover, I felt like I was failing to live up to my responsibility as a food writer to seek out little-known restaurants and unfamiliar dishes. Hong Kong welcomes 36 *million* tourists per year, most of whom stick to a small area in the central part of town, and the city is famous for Cantonese food, arguably the most well-known cuisine in the world. Eaters here post hundreds of reviews a day on Openrice, the local equivalent of Yelp, in English and Chinese. Hong Kong is the beaten path.

In other words, I fell into a classic tourist trap: seeking an imaginary *real* Hong Kong while the real thing was right in front of me all along. (Hmm, isn't this also a classic romantic comedy plot?) Getting squished at a crowded pedestrian crossing is something that would definitely happen in Tokyo, but on Nathan Road in Kowloon, your transitory mob will include locals, tourists from fifty countries, and businesspeople from every inhabited continent, a level of diversity I've never seen in Tokyo.

The tourist-infested Peak Tram is the real Hong Kong, and so is the Ocean Park amusement park, where the Arctic Blast roller coaster offers a fleeting glimpse of the quintessential HK view: apartment towers overlooking the South China Sea.

Only a real asshole would brood over not being the first person to write about a rare dumpling, and I got over myself after a couple of days, in time to thoroughly enjoy a meal at a chain restaurant at a mall. As Iris and I shared a steamer of soup dumplings and a plate of spicy stir-fried pork, I realized we were having a really good time.

So this is the story of our week in Hong Kong, bug bites and all.

A bit of a rough neighborhood

"So what do you think?" said Masterson. He was standing by the open window, looking down into the noise and traffic of Nathan Road.

"Can't fault the location," I said.
                                        —John Lanchester

Remember the guy who came into town on the Star Ferry? Well, you should do that. We took the bus.

As the double-decker A21 bus rolled across the Tsing Ma bridge, Iris leaned on my shoulder. Like any dad, I pointed out the world's most obvious sights. There's a mountain! There's a skyscraper! From our second-floor perch, we watched a very Hong Kong block of identical 30-story apartment towers scroll past.

The A21 continued past Tsing Yi, a tiny island crammed with apartment towers, and onto the Kowloon peninsula. We passed Stonecutter's Island, once a standalone island, now absorbed into a nearby landmass by land reclamation.

(The number of standalone islands in Hong Kong has, for this reason, been shrinking for over a century.)

The boundary between Kowloon and the New Territories is conveniently called Boundary Street. As we approached it, Iris said, "Now we're really in the city."

"Almost," I promised. Coming into Hong Kong is like walking from the shallow to the deep end of a swimming pool. Just when you think the landscape can't get any more up-to-the-neck urban, it does.

We drove down Nathan Road through Mong Kok, Hong Kong's most densely populated neighborhood. The main street of Kowloon, Nathan Road is a boulevard and a bazaar, Hong Kong's urban Grand Canyon, lined with ten-story apartments and guesthouses, karaoke parlors and pawnshops, fast-food restaurants and five-star hotels. The bus dropped us off in front of a clothing store called LOG-IN in a neighborhood called Yau Ma Tei, and we were in Hong Kong.

My wife Laurie told a Hong Kong-born coworker, Ms. Fong, about our trip. "Where are they staying?" she asked.

"I don't remember the name, but it's near the Temple Street Night Market," replied Laurie.

"Hmm, that's a bit of a rough neighborhood," said Ms. Fong. "Well, at least they'll be able to see the real Hong Kong."

Our landlord, Stanley, met us on Shanghai Street in front of Man Ming Court. Hong Kong is full of Courts and Mansions, none of which deliver on the imperial grandeur suggested by their names. The entrance to Man Ming Court is a metal door, incised by mail slots, standing between two restaurant supply shops. We found Stanley and his court on Airbnb.com.

Stanley produced a massive key ring to rival any janitor's. As Iris and I gaped, he methodically thumbed through the keys for several minutes. Cars and double-deckers and minibuses streamed by. The air was warm and humid and carried that Southeast Asian cocktail of tropical fruit and diesel fumes. Groups of young people walked by, chatting and laughing and playing with their phones.

"Aha," he said finally, and let us in.

Like many big-city apartment buildings, Man Ming Court has a whiff of the tragedy of the commons about it. The stairwell is dim and flecked with chipped paint and floor tiles. Tenants put their trash bags out on the landing. As Iris and I trudged upstairs after Stanley, I was concerned: misled by Photoshopped real estate photos, I'd brought my only child to a tenement flophouse.

Stanley showed us the security gate over the apartment door, which was not reassuring, especially when he explained that it didn't lock. So we'd be safe from animals without opposable thumbs. Except velociraptors.

Then we stepped inside. The apartment was lovely. It looked just like on the website: a bright living room, a well-stocked kitchenette, and a bedroom with comfortable beds for each of us. Each room boasted a powerful air conditioner. The kitchen window overlooked the exuberant neon sign of the Shun Cheong Pawn Shop, which bathed the bedroom in an orange glow each night until it clicked off at 9:45 p.m. We dropped our luggage and headed out into Kowloon, the night air thick with humidity and the tonal syllables of Cantonese.

A trip to Hong Kong reveals the extent to which Cantonese has become part of the non-Chinese-speaking world. The name of your favorite Chinese-American (or Chinese-Canadian, or Chinese-British) restaurant, if it's not called "Lucky Phoenix" or the like, is probably written in Hong Kong–style romanized Cantonese. The Hong Kong map is a multilingual stew of British and Chinese influence. We often found ourselves standing at the corner of Reclamation Street and Hi Lung Lane, or traveling between Causeway Bay and Sheung Wan.

Before the trip, Iris's friend Alex, who speaks Cantonese, took me aside. "Is it true you're going to Hong Kong?" he asked. I told him yes. "I've never been, but I have family there," he said, and suggested that we might just run into members of his family and recognize them. Then Alex offered his sagest advice. "Don't ever sing a song in Chinese. You'll get it all wrong because of the *tones.*" He grabbed his hair and walked away.

Iris and I rounded the corner to the **Temple Street Night Market**, which sets up every night at around 7 p.m. on a ten-block stretch of its eponymous street. It's a flea market selling clothing, souvenirs, electronics, jewelry, and, to Iris's delight, knockoff Lego sets. She selected a small set, and I gave her thirty-five Hong Kong dollars and a long lecture about the up- and downsides of intellectual property law. (Not really.)

The exchange rate between Hong Kong and U.S. dollars is pegged at 7.75 HKD to 1 USD, so 35 HKD is about 4.50 USD. As Hong Kong uses the same dollar sign as the U.S. and Canada, we quickly got used to spending $65 for breakfast and $7.50 for a pack of tissues. It was like adjusting to a new pair of glasses, and when we got home we had to adjust all over again: at the Vancouver airport I spent $10 Canadian for some candy and mixed nuts and didn't realized I'd been fleeced until after we were on the plane. From here on, prices are in U.S. dollars, except when I say otherwise.

Inexpensive restaurants cluster around the market, sprawling out onto Temple Street and its side streets. They specialize in noodles, spicy crab, rice plates. Iris and I selected a place with roast meats hanging in the window,

Ming Kee Chicken Congee. We sat indoors, enjoying a bit of air conditioning and sharing a combo plate of BBQ pork and roast duck with rice and *gai lan* (Chinese broccoli). "Hey, it's saucy rice, just the way I like it," said Iris. Indeed, our rice was drizzled with seasoned soy sauce. I'm always telling Iris not to pour soy sauce on her rice at restaurants (although now that I say this, why do I care?). Here, they did it for her.

When we got back to the apartment, I crashed out immediately. Iris stayed up reading Wizard of Oz books until well after the Shun Cheong Pawn Shop sign went to sleep.

The smell of fear

We met friend-of-a-friend Teresa Kuan at a local chain called **Honeymoon Dessert**. On the way, we blundered into a private party at a fancy dim sum parlor called, no joke, The Grand Stage. We had to retreat down a back stairway that screamed "do not enter." This kind of thing happens to me a lot, usually when I'm really, absolutely sure I'm going the right way.

Honeymoon specializes in puddings and custards, multifarious and gelatinous: sago and grass jelly, tofu and red bean, coconut milk and sesame soup. Everything on the menu features at least one element that will freak out the average hot fudge sundae lover. An entire section is devoted to "sweet balls."

I ordered tofu pudding with coconut milk and fresh mango. Teresa had a mango-sago combo. Sago is a starch made from palm tree trunks, a staple food in New Guinea and made into tapioca-like pearls for consumption everywhere else. Iris sussed out a scoop of plain vanilla ice cream. The waitress raised an eyebrow at this. Not green tea ice cream? Nothing jellied?

Nearby, people were eating durian. It might have been Double Durian in Vanilla Sauce, or Durian Pancake, both actual menu items.

Iris held her nose stridently. "They should have a separate section for people eating durian. You know, like a smoking section. For durian." She was not joking.

"They don't actually serve that much durian here," said Teresa. "It just smells like it." Teresa is a professor of anthropology, working on a book about the history of parenting guides. My books are, thankfully, not serious enough to merit her attention.

I sank into my seat. This was our first full day in Hong Kong, and I was homesick and overheated, jet lag and a lingering airplane sleep cramp settling around the side of my neck like a Vulcan nerve pinch. Iris was, as always, a diplomatic cream puff. She calibrated herself to Hong Kong Time like a Shenzhen-built smartphone, instantly and without drama.

So I sat quietly, on the verge of nodding off, while Iris and Teresa chatted about Chinese and Japanese food and how to cook an eel. Then my tofu pudding arrived. I'm a big fan of tofu and firmly in the let-tofu-be-tofu camp. Don't blend it into smoothies or make it into fake hot dogs. For tofu pudding, however, I make an exception. Tofu pudding is simply very soft silken tofu, usually served with a sweet syrup (almond is classic). Here it was mixed with coconut milk and topped with cubes of fresh mango. The coconut milk and tofu were both soft and white, but with different and complementary textures that blended as my spoon coaxed them together. With each bite, I became more human.

On the way home we crossed the north end of the Temple Street Night Market, where a vendor had set out piles of spiky fruit. "Oh, god, *more* durian?" moaned Iris.

I'd eaten durian before and have yet to acquire the taste. "I kind of like the smell, though," I said.

"Traitor."

Tea and toast

The restaurant gave its English name as Delicious Catering. Boring. I made a grand translation of the characters of its Chinese name (味皇): Emperor of Flavor.

Emperor of Flavor is a *cha chaan teng* chain. A cha chaan teng, aside from being a phrase that makes Autocorrect furious (did you mean "chat chain tent"?), is a Hong Kong diner. They're cheap, casual places, open all day, especially good for breakfast. A cloud of cigarette smoke would seem right at home in a cha chaan teng, and it was until 2007, when Hong Kong banned smoking in restaurants.

In a city of fusion, breakfast is Hong Kong's most cross-cultural meal. It's also egalitarian. You see fancy men in business suits, tourists, housekeepers, and college kids piled into the same diner, drinking tea and eating eggs and toast and macaroni soup, a flavorless concoction whose popularity is hard to understand.

If you like greasy breakfasts, you will love Hong Kong. Iris and I each ordered a French toast combo meal: a slice of French toast, scrambled eggs, and choice of meat. I asked for the pork cutlet and Iris had the fish cutlet. Each plate was under $4.

The portions were massive. My pork, in particular, schnitzeled out beyond the edge of the plate. And everything was well-seasoned, crisp and just greasy enough. I kind of wished I was hung over.

Hong Kong French toast bears little resemblance to anything you'll find in the U.S. (or France). Two pieces of white bread are glued together with peanut butter, deep-fried, and served with butter and honey. It's exactly as ridiculous as it sounds, and I recommend it, although perhaps not every day. Iris and I were so enamored of Emperor of Flavor, however, that we went back the next day, hoping to score a booth.

We scored a booth, but this being Hong Kong, we sat on the same side of the booth because we were sharing it with two strangers. The city's tiny restaurants couldn't survive if they let two diners monopolize a four-top, so we shared tables often. As you might imagine, the protocol in this situation is to smile politely and then pretend your neighbors don't exist.

On our second visit to Emperor of Flavor, Iris and I shared a single pork cutlet combo. There was no third visit. That's how a deep-fried French toast fling works: you go from "This is genius!" to "Okay, I get it," in no time. I assume locals who eat French toast a lot have iron constitutions, work construction, or get sent to Japan to work in the sumo industry.

With our breakfast combo, I ordered Hong Kong milk tea. At home in Seattle, Laurie drinks black tea with milk. I drink green tea. Neither of us will go near the other's tea. She thinks green tea tastes like leftover water from boiling spinach. I think milky black tea is for English grannies.

(I have nothing against English grannies except as culinary role models.)

In Hong Kong, however, I drank milk tea, which is brewed in a preposterous manner. Brew some very strong black tea (Lipton is typical), boiling the tea leaves for several minutes until you have an inky, astringent liquor. Then strain it through a fine mesh cloth and mix it with heated evaporated milk. Sugar is optional; I skip it.

I wasn't just drinking milk tea to fit in with the locals. I *loved* it. The tea is so strong, it's like espresso, a slap upside the head of English Breakfast. This stuff is highly caffeinated and intense, with a bitter edge that cuts through the blanket of evaporated milk.

You don't have to eat at a cha chaan teng to get your milk tea fix. Most noodle shops and congee stalls and dim sum places also serve it. Some restaurants also offer *yuan yang,* which is milk tea mixed with coffee in unequal proportions, about two-thirds tea and one-third coffee. This is as good a metaphor as any for Hong Kong's melting pot, although the population of Hong Kong is close to 95% ethnic Chinese.

I tried yuan yang, expecting to hate it, and thoroughly enjoyed the stuff. The coffee flavor hits first, then the sonorous swell of tea drowns out the coffee. Now I want to try blending up all sorts of unlikely breakfast cocktails. Prune juice latte, anyone?

French toast is secondary in the realm of Hong Kong's English-derived toast obsession. We had breakfast one day at a Singaporean chain, Toast Box, where Iris and I each ordered a version of classic thick toast, an inch-thick slice of toast, usually slathered with salted butter or peanut butter. The toast itself is white bread similar to Japan's *shokupan* or America's Texas toast. Iris's buttered toast arrived cut into nine squares ("Like a tic-tac-toe board," she noted) and served with toothpicks as utensils. I ordered kaya toast. Kaya is coconut jam, hailing from Malaysia but very popular in Hong Kong. It's essentially lemon curd made with coconut milk instead of lemon juice, rich, sweet, and thick. Kaya toast, thickly buttered before receiving a layer of jam, is wonderful with unsweetened milk tea.

"I'd like something more savory for breakfast," said Iris after a couple of days of toast. So we wandered around the corner from our apartment to a place called **Famous Beef Brisket Noodles**.

All over Asia, people start the day with steaming hot noodle soups. I've had memorable noodle breakfasts of *kuaytiaw* in Thailand, soba in Japan, and now wonton noodles in Hong Kong. Actually, it was Iris who ordered the wonton noodles at Famous Beef Brisket. We sat across from a businessman wolfing down soupless brisket noodles. He finished just as Iris's wonton noodles arrived.

Wonton noodles are one of Hong Kong's favorite foods, eaten three meals a day. Over on Island side, two renowned wonton noodle shops, Tsim Chai Kee and Mak's, square off across Wellington Street. Mak's is so famous that it has its own Wikipedia page (http://en.wikipedia.org/wiki/Mak's_Noodle). It's not necessary to go to a famous place for wonton noodles, however, any more than you have to go to one one particular hot dog stand in New York.

Eating in Hong Kong is about more than what's on your plate at any given meal. It's about stepping into a vernacular food culture of congee, roast duck, thick toast, dim sum, wonton noodles, Chinese broccoli, and stir-fried everything. I didn't grow up in that kind of food culture, and

I suspect few Americans do unless they live in New Orleans or a close-knit immigrant community. Every so often the food writers of Seattle will argue over whether there exists such as thing as Pacific Northwest cuisine. I'm in the "no" camp: there's cedar-planked salmon, chicken teriyaki, and...what else?

If you come from a place without a vernacular food culture, it's a peculiar joy to visit one, an immersion school for the palate. Iris's wonton noodles were part of the Hong Kong food pantheon: very thin, chewy egg noodles in fish broth, garnished with a few scallions and topped with six plump shrimp wontons. The noodles are barely cooked, designed to soak up enough hot broth to become edible by the time the broth has cooled enough to slurp. The wontons feature slippery wrappers and big chunks of tender shrimp. It's a noodle-on-noodle melange that makes about as much sense in theory as combining tea and coffee, but is brilliant in practice.

I ordered the same dish but with Chiuchow-style fish dumplings. The Chiuchow people (also frequently written as Teochew or Chaozhou) come from Guangzhou province, adjacent to Hong Kong, and Chiuchow immigrants have profoundly influenced Hong Kong cuisine. Chiuchow cuisine has given Hong Kong these fish dumplings—chewy skins enveloping satisfyingly bouncy fish mousse—as well as oyster omelets and many other popular dishes.

These noodle soups demand a bit of chile paste, which is always found on the table.

Fortified with breakfast, Iris and I headed off for the wildest public transit line on earth.

On the up and up

We came into the harbor an hour after dawn. The last shreds of mist clinging to the Peak were being burned off by the sun; they looked like smoke, as if the island were an active volcano.

—*John Lanchester*

Iris brought a small point and shoot camera to Hong Kong with the intention of shooting a ton of photos. She took five pictures on our first morning, including this one of me on Nathan Road in Kowloon.

CHILD OCTOPUS

Then she got bored and put the camera away for the rest of the week. One night, however, we were hanging out with our friend Dana on a roof garden in Central. Iris borrowed my camera to snap a photo of IFC Two, Hong Kong's second-tallest building. Naturally, it came out better than any picture I've ever taken.

"It totally looked like there should be lightning crackling around the top and an evil villain cackling," Iris said later.

You can't see it in the photo, but behind IFC Two looms a broad-shouldered presence, much taller than any building in town. It's called Victoria Peak, or more often just "the Peak." It's long been the haunt of Hong Kong's rich and famous, but you can climb the Peak in more style than a Rolls-Royce by taking the Peak Tram.

The Peak Tram is a funicular, a mountain railway, which has been ferrying passengers up and down the Peak since 1888. Iris and I waited in a short line and boarded the tram in the morning. The ascent begins slowly, then accelerates to an improbably high speed. It's like the first half of a rollercoaster ride, if a negligent carny leaned on the throttle. The tram makes a couple of sharp turns on the way to the top, and several times Iris said, "This. Is. AWESOME!" Or maybe that was me. At its steepest, the Peak Tram climbs a 48 percent grade, far steeper than any road in the world.

Halfway up, the tram affords riders a view of the skyline, unnervingly askew. When you're riding uphill at such an angle, your brain rebels. *Hey, buddy,* it says. *You're the normal one. Everyone else is tilted.* Tram riders have been observing this since Hong Kong built its first tall buildings. British author Martin Booth lived on the Peak with his family in the 1950s and rode the tram often enough that he got bored—until the day he shared the ride with Clark Gable.

Back then, the tram was used by local residents to get around. Nowadays, locals go by bus or car, and the tram is crammed with tourists. If you want to ride it at night, you'll queue up. At the top, the tram dumps you directly into the gift shop and then into a mall. Iris and I wandered around for quite a while trying to figure out how to get outside, because our overlords were trying to lead us to a paid viewing gallery. We finally found the way out and explored the free outdoor viewpoint, where a woman took our picture and asked us which cruise ship we'd arrived on.

And that, my friends, that toxic veil over the city, is the tragedy of Hong Kong. At night, the view from the Peak is of a glittering, otherworldly metropolis, all the promise of human potential realized in steel and glass and electric light. By day, the city is nearly invisible, shrouded in a haze of boat and car and factory exhaust.

We wandered around for a little while and stopped at a bubble tea stand featuring a drink machine with twin warning labels:

DON'T PUT YOUR HANDS INSIDE THE MACHINE WHEN THE POWER IS ON

DON'T PUT HAND INTO THE MACHINE UNLESS THE POWER IS TURNED OFF

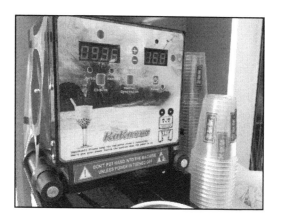

Would somebody please send help? I'm on top of the Peak with my hand stuck in a bubble tea machine.

Hong Kong is probably the world capital of unnecessary warning signs and recorded messages. Don't step onto a boat if it's pitching heavily. Don't climb over this fence. Don't play in the fountain. Use caution when exiting the lift. Sometimes I entertained myself by imagining that I was the guy who actually needed all these reminders.

"Oh, cool, we get to sit backwards," said Iris, using caution while entering the tram for the return trip.

After hobnobbing with cruise people on the Peak, Iris and I walked from the Lower Terminus to Des Voeux Road, where double-decker electric trams ply the street along the north shore of Hong Kong Island. En route, we stumbled upon a protest march. It had something to do with children, but we couldn't figure out what it was about, even though most of the signs were in English. Parents marched with kids on their shoulders and signs calling for the protection of "our topkids," whatever that means. So far, China has kept its promise to maintain "One Country, Two Systems." Hong Kong has freedom of speech, press, assembly, and internet access. Even so, getting involved in a protest in Hong Kong seemed like a really bad idea, and I was relieved when we parted ways.

More than any other place but Venice, Hong Kong's transit is entertainment: a visitor could easily ride the subway, Peak Tram, ferry, double-decker bus, aerial cable car, and street tram in the same day. Iris tapped her Child Octopus card and we climbed the stairs to the upper level of the street tram.

Unlike the Peak Tram, the trams of Des Voeux Road are very much used by locals. They're cheap, charming, and slow, often bunching up three or four strong at stoplights. We slid along for a couple of stops and arrived at the base of yet another way to get up the Peak: the Mid-Levels Escalator.

The Mid-Levels Escalator is the world's longest escalator complex. It runs up the slope of Victoria Peak through the Soho and Mid-Levels neighborhoods for about half a mile, cutting a perpendicular swath across dozens of small streets, each sporting shops, restaurants, *dai pai dong* street food stalls, butchers, and vegetable sellers.

To be clear, this is not a tram, a streetcar, or any other kind of vehicle. It's just a huge-ass escalator, exactly like the kind you take at the mall, running one story above the street with landings at every intersection. The escalator runs downhill in the morning for commuters coming down the mountain and uphill the rest of the day, because the Peak is really, really steep, and the whole point of the escalator is to encourage people to shop and eat at higher altitudes than they'd typically ascend to on foot.

At one point, the escalator opens directly into the second floor of a PARKnSHOP supermarket, where we bought a couple of German Kinder Joy candies, ate them at a covered rest area, and assembled the included plastic toys. (There are PARKnSHOP locations all over Hong Kong; we never saw one with a parking lot.)

Although it's lit up at night and serves some of HK's wealthiest neighborhoods, the escalator is anything but deluxe: it's well-worn (55,000 people ride it daily) and feels like a reliable old Honda Civic. Its segments are a mixture of stair-step escalators and inclined moving walkways called "travelators."

As a people mover, the escalator works like a streetcar: not built for long distance travel but for extending your walk beyond the point where you'd usually poop out. By now, we were several hundred feet up, sweaty, tired, our breakfast of toast and eggs and milk tea long digested. "What do you want for lunch?" I asked.

"How about dim sum?" said Iris.

So we hiked down the stairs and found some.

Yum cha

Everything in China stops for food.
                    —Christopher Knowles

Iris and I took our seats at a big round table at Luk Yu Teahouse and began selecting dishes from a long menu of buns, dumplings, and their allies.

Ten-year-old me would love Hong Kong unreservedly, because dim sum is everywhere. If you love ordering dim sum from rumbling metal carts, you'll be disappointed to learn that carts have disappeared from the vast majority of Hong Kong dim sum houses. That means giving up on serendipity, yes, but it also means avoiding the inevitable tragedy of cart-based dim sum: waiting half an hour hoping for har gow, only to see them go by right after you pay the check. I don't miss the carts.

Luk Yu features classic dim sum items and the kind of efficient Chinese restaurant service that could easily be mistaken for surly. It took me and Iris a while to figure out that if you need a waiter in Hong Kong, it's polite (and necessary) to wave them over with a loud *m'goi,* which is the word for both "excuse me" and "thank you."

Iris was on a mission: find the best version of her favorite dim sum dish, leaf-wrapped sticky rice. Here it was steamed with bits of roast duck. I burned my fingers unwrapping the dried lotus leaf to reveal a glutinous mass of rice and meat. (Iris pulled out her camera but was too busy admiring her snapshots to capture my pain.)

"Oh, this is GOOD," said Iris, scooping some rice out of the leaf. I agreed. Sticky rice is tricky rice, and this dish got it right, well-seasoned and studded throughout with bits of flavorful duck and shrimp. The rest of the meal was perfunctory, but we were restored.

For dessert, we walked down the block to **Tai Cheong** bakery, maker of the most famous egg tarts in town. Egg tarts (*daan taat*) are individual pastries, always served hot, with a sweet, tender crust and a smooth, custardy egg filling. We failed to understand the lure of the egg tart on the first try. Why not serve it at room temperature? Why was the crust so sweet? Why does the filling taste a little like an omelet?

So I was prepared to file egg tarts away in the lobe of my brain reserved for Asian desserts I don't understand, along with India's gulab jamun, Japan's red bean paste, and most of the menu at Honeymoon Dessert. Then, a couple of days later, we passed another Tai Cheong location on the way to the ferry. "I'm going to get another one of those egg tarts," I said. Iris shrugged. We split the tart in half. Crumbs flew everywhere.

"Actually, this thing is good," allowed Iris. "Okay, it's really good." After that I kept threatening to detour for egg tarts every time we went out. "You are NOT getting another egg tart," said Iris.

"Why not?" I asked.

There is no good answer.

Luk Yu only whetted our appetites for dim sum, so we were pleased when Gary Lim and Fiona Cheng invited us to meet them at a high-end Island-side teahouse, **Fu Sing Shark Fin Seafood Restaurant**. Gary owns a printing company and comes off as the successful businessmen that he is. He wore a dark, well-tailored suit. I was wearing a plaid shirt and carrying a camera, and Iris was wearing shorts. Yokel chic? Despite the fact that he and Fiona should have refused to be seen in public with us, they ordered a dozen dishes at Fu Sing. "You guys have small appetites," said Fiona when we failed to finish everything.

In case you're not sure what to order, Fu Sing has large wall-mounted monitors showing some of their most popular dishes, including glistening glamor shots of roast pork and BBQ pork. Both are meats you see hanging in windows all over Hong Kong along with roast ducks and geese, and both are delicious. Roast pork, in its HK incarnation, is a refined dish made of nothing but pork belly and salt. The goal is to achieve thin, crispy skin and tender meat, and it's often cut into perfect squares for serving. BBQ pork is its lusty cousin, dyed red and dripping with sweet glaze.

Gary kept ordering. I mentioned that I was craving vegetables after a couple of days of meat- and starch-heavy meals, and he ordered greens in shrimp paste, served sizzling in a cast-iron dish. Gary stirred it together and offered me the fragrant leaves. It was hot, salty, and umami-rich, but what really brought the dish together was the texture, perfectly tender to the core. I was about to praise the skill of the cook who prepared this napa cabbage, but as I finished chewing, I realized, *wait a minute, that texture is familiar.* "This is lettuce, isn't it?" I asked.

"Romaine," confirmed Gary.

A waiter set down a plate of *char siu bao,* baked BBQ pork buns. Unlike the smooth, glossy tops of the buns we'd had at Luk Yu, these had a matte finish and were crusted with a paper-thin layer of sugar. Gary explained that one successful dim sum restaurant had started serving char siu bao in this style a few years back and has been widely copied. I liked the crisp texture and the balance between the sweet topping and sweet filling; Iris, who loves dessert but wants it to stay away from her lunch, was unimpressed.

One morning in Yau Ma Tei, we intended to have breakfast at Famous Beef Brisket Noodle, but Iris eyed the place next door. "Actually, I could go for some dim sum," she said. So we sat down at **Fu Kee Delicious Food**. Again, Iris went straight for the sticky rice, and she received the most exuberant version yet, with a mix of chicken, pork, Chinese sausage, and Spam.

"You want to try our special har gow?" asked the proprietor.

Did I ever.

A Kowloon kind of girl

"Yes, Hong Kong has many people. Mong Kok. So terrible."

"I love Mong Kok,"she said.
                              —PJ Converse

People in Hong Kong tend to identify with Island-side or Kowloon-side, based on where they live or where they grew up. Islanders are famously reluctant to cross the harbor, even though it's a three-minute ride on the MTR.

From afar, I found this petty neighborhood nationalism puzzling. That's the thing about ingroup/outgroup dichotomies: they all seem silly until you're in one of the groups. Once we moved into our Yau Ma Tei walkup, Iris and I became die-hard Kowloon types. We walked up and down massive Nathan Road, watching double-deckers go by. "Check this out," said Iris, showing Laurie the photos she shot in front of Toast Box. "One bus. Another bus. AN-OTHER bus. There are SO many buses." We nabbed the coveted seats at the front of the upper level a couple of times, and it was like a toddler's conception of driving a bus: you just giggle and bounce in your seat and point at stuff, and the bus drives itself.

We lived in the heart of the restaurant supply district on Shanghai Street, and Iris befriended the shop cats at two nearby stores, including the famous **Chan Chi Kee Cutlery**. Better known as CCK, the shop sells inexpensive and high-quality Chinese cleavers in every possible size, along with woks, spatulas, and skimmers. These cleavers look like a VW bus but handle like a Ferrari. When Martin Yan dismantles a chicken in eighteen seconds, he uses a Chinese cleaver.

While I browsed the cutting boards, polished six-inch-thick cross sections of tree trunks, Iris petted the tiny tabby on the front counter. One of CCK's cats curled up and used my shoe as a pillow. I think this was Iris's favorite part of the whole trip. "Dada, give me the camera NOW," she said.

Down the block, a couple of girls about Iris's age were waiting for the bus with their dad. They rolled up on their

Razor scooters, hopped off, cuddled a cat, and took off just in time to board the number 3 minibus.

Walking down Man Ming Lane, we were stopped by the aroma of freshly made egg waffles. Made on a waffle iron with a grid of semi-circular divots, egg waffles look like bubble wrap made of dough. We ordered a waffle, and the guy in line behind us said something to the cook. "I asked them to make you a fresh one," the guy explained. We thanked him and headed home with a steaming waffle, tearing it up into sweet, crusty, coconut-scented ingots.

The next morning, of course, we wanted egg waffles for breakfast. I walked over to the same stand, and a couple others. No egg waffles yet. They must be more of an afternoon snack. I came back with sweet, flaky pineapple buns instead. These contain no pineapple; they're named for the sugar-crusted top, which looks like the skin of a pineapple. We held a pineapple bun taste-off, a local bakery pitted against 7-Eleven.

Yes, 7-Eleven was superior.

I've heard Hong Kong tourists complain that the place is too Western, that after 150 years of British occupation and another decade or two of exuberant capitalism, it's no different from visiting New York. It's true that Hong Kong is a crossroads, and that its neon signs are more likely to be hawking Coach or Hermès than any homegrown brand. (Although every bus carries ads for the local Chow Tai Fook jewelry chain.) But I suspect the complaint comes from visitors who failed to spend enough time in Kowloon. Or, to be more cynical about it, it comes from visitors who equate poverty with authenticity.

In his book *Gweilo,* Martin Booth recalls wandering the Kowloon streets of the 1950s as an independent eight-year-old. He eats street food, chats with locals, and picks up a working knowledge of Cantonese. Booth's Kowloon is immediately recognizable to a visitor of today. It's safe, life spills out onto the streets, and it has a small town big city feel. Then, as now, buildings under construction are clad in bamboo scaffolding, instantly recognizable and stronger than it looks.

Iris and I dropped our laundry at a little storefront on Reclamation Street and passed a snack shop on the way to the Wellcome Supermarket in Prosperous Garden. (Sometimes I popped into the snack shop in the afternoon for a bun or fish balls.) Inside the supermarket, roast meat glistened in the display window at the meat counter, just like at any BBQ shop. Hong Kong's small urban supermarkets stock an appealing mix of European, Japanese, Chinese, and North American goods, Earl Grey juxtaposed with oolong, dragonfruit alongside Washington apples.

"My brain is just starting to adjust to the idea that we're really in Hong Kong," said Iris after a couple of days. Within another day or two, she was starting to refer to our little place in Yau Ma Tei as home, even though the humidity was punishing and the local insects kept biting her legs.

"Hey, is that a new bug bite or a scab?" I asked.

Iris checked her leg. "Oh, that's dried soy sauce."

My brain never successfully adjusted to written Chinese. I can read Japanese, and Chinese uses many of the same characters. It also uses many additional characters, uses them in different ways, and in general conspires to give a Japanese speaker a case of situational dyslexia.

Luckily, nearly every restaurant in central Hong Kong and Kowloon has an English menu. Still, I was thrilled when we came upon a place called 美味餃子店. In Japanese and Chinese alike, there's no doubt that this means "delicious dumpling shop." The menu is vestigial: dumplings fried, boiled, or in soup, flavored with garlic chives or "cabbage patch." The fried dumplings are half-moons, crisped on both sides, and filled with well-seasoned pork and greens. The dumplings in soup present a worthwhile chopstick challenge, satisfyingly slippery and meaty.

At a Circle-K convenience store next to the dumpling place, Iris asked me for fifteen Hong Kong dollars to buy a plastic toy from a machine. "I don't think——" I started to say.

"Dada, you're going to want to see this," she said. The machine, a Japanese *gachapon* dispenser, was full of hyperrealistic toy miniatures of European baked goods: croissant, brioche, pretzel, Pullman loaf. I handed over the coins.

That night, Iris and I were struck with twin rice cravings. She wanted *cheung fan,* stuffed rice noodle rolls with sweet soy sauce, sort of like Chinese enchiladas. I was after congee, rice porridge. We searched for a place that offered both and ended up back at Ming Kee Chicken Congee, where we'd eaten roast meats on our first night in town. Iris's cheung fan were hot and slippery, filled with braised beef brisket and dripping with soy sauce and meat juices.

May we talk about congee for a moment? Known as *jook* in Cantonese, congee is rice porridge. Like noodles, it can be eaten at any time of day but is especially popular for breakfast and late nights.

Congee hasn't yet made the leap to the English side of the Chinese-American restaurant menu. Dim sum's appeal is immediately obvious to people who didn't grow up with it. Congee, meanwhile, is gray and watery, deficient in texture and flavor alike, popular among babies and other toothless people.

And I wanted it, bad. Congee is warm, soothing, studded with tangy bits of pickled greens, nubs of bone-in chicken or slices of fish, sometimes a few salted peanuts. It's also served lawsuit-inducingly hot. I wanted to get with the soothing goodness, already, but I kept burning the roof of my mouth.

I offered Iris a bite of congee. "Nah, I'm okay," she said, a rice noodle sliding off her chopsticks. That's okay. It's never too late to adopt a new comfort food.

Water, water, everywhere, and...

Iris and I quickly acclimated to two unfamiliar aspects of Hong Kong restaurant service. I've already mentioned that when you want a waiter, you wave one over. HK has none of this "and how are we enjoying everything?" business. Good riddance.

We learned to carry our own paper napkins, because restaurants rarely supply them. You buy the napkins—facial tissues, really—in pocket packs at convenience stores or drugstores. They come in a variety of scents, including jasmine, applewood, citrus, and unscented, charmingly known as "neutral."

What we never got used to was the water situation.

If you're reading this somewhere other than the United States, know that Americans have this weird habit. We like to drink lots of ice water with meals. Not just cold water, water with plenty of ice cubes melting into it to keep it at a brisk 0.1 °C. We expect ice water to be provided at the beginning of the meal without asking, at no charge, and to be refilled promptly whenever the glass is getting low. This is all covered in the Bill of Rights.

Nobody else in the world seems to share our water hangups. In most cities, you can get ice water by asking nicely. In Hong Kong, however, drinking ice water with meals is just not done. When we asked for it, waiters generally reacted as if we'd gone into an American restaurant and requested a mug of piping hot Budweiser.

Bottled water at vending machines and convenience stores is not quite as cold as the American palate demands. To top it off, the refrigerator in our apartment maxed out (minned out?) at about $8°c$.

At one restaurant, we asked for ice water and received glasses of hot water. At a dumpling restaurant in Mong Kok, the waiter said, "We don't have that. You want cold soy milk?" We did. It was delicious.

We were getting a little desperate. We started carrying our own bottle of water into restaurants, like a drunk with a hip flask. Hong Kong is located just south of the Tropic of Cancer. Its climate is technically subtropical, but tell that to our fragile, pampered bodies. Iris developed a pastiche of heat rashes. "It wasn't very reassuring when you got back and said, 'Now you can see all of Iris's assorted rashes,'" said Laurie.

We know that there is no physiological need to drink ice-cold beverages in hot weather, but the longer we went without them, the more we craved them. One afternoon we wandered past a tropical fruit stand called **King of Coconut** with a sign promising ICE CANE JUICE next to a pile of green sugarcane stalks. The woman behind the counter cut several stalks in half lengthwise with a cleaver and fed them into a juicer that resembled a wood chipper. It chewed through the stalks, dispensing the juice, while the spent, squeezed cane emerged flat and fibrous. Amazingly, there was no DO NOT STICK ARM INTO MACHINE label.

Grinning, the woman passed us the cup of cane juice. It was opaque and yellow with a bit of a foamy head, an initial hit of fruit, and a pure sucrose aftertaste. It was not, however, iced. It was warm. Iris was furious. "But it SAID ice cane juice!" she wailed.

Whenever possible, I'd stop off at a chain called **Hui Lau Shan**, which specializes in tropical fruit drinks. The mango smoothie is made with plenty of fresh mango, and more to the point is blended with *actual ice cubes.*

Finally, Iris and I cracked the cold drink code. We met our friends Dana and Yan for dinner in Causeway Bay, a busy Island-side neighborhood with an appealing pedestrian shopping district. We arrived early and Iris discovered a play area festooned with foam sculptures of food, including a doughnut carousel.

"I must confess that I am not the biggest food expert around," wrote Dana when I emailed her to ask if we could meet for dinner. Naturally, she took us to our two favorite restaurants of the trip. We walked around the corner from the doughnut to **Du Lac Bleu** for clay pot rice. (Why this place has a French name, I have no idea.)

We could smell the clay pot rice before we got to the restaurant, because the clay pots cook on a stove out front. Each individual-sized pot is filled with rice, topped with meat and vegetables, covered and cooked over a flame until the bottom of the rice chars and crisps up. It's the southern Chinese equivalent of Korean *dolsot bibimbap,* but because the pot is covered for the final minutes of cooking, smoke rises from the sizzling rice and perfumes the toppings, especially the cabbage.

Iris ordered pork ribs and chicken feet, and I had black bean sauce eel with Chinese sausage. Iris had never tried chicken feet before, and I beamed. Then I un-beamed when she received her food and said, "On second thought, those are a little too orange for me," and transferred her chicken feet to my bowl with her chopsticks.

Iris was thrilled that diners are encouraged to pour soy sauce all over their rice before digging in. Clay pot rice is wonderful: piping hot, smoky, and fragrant. My cabbage was crisp and infused with smoke. (Iris's cabbage, which she gifted to me, was also crisp and infused with smoke.) The main event, of course, is the crusty rice bottom, which peels off in large pieces. The classic combination is chicken and Chinese sausage, and both Dana and Yan ordered it, but you really can't go wrong with any topping. Eel has a bit of a deep-sea funk to it that I always want to describe as "earthy," even though that can't be right, and it pairs well with the sweet sausage and salty fermented black beans.

"As you can see, eating is basically what we do here,"

said Dana. She and Yan started reeling off recommendations: dim sum, congee, cha chaan teng.

"You know cha chaan teng?" asked Yan. "This place is kind of like a cha chaan teng but a little more upscale." I looked around and tried not to laugh. Du Lac Bleu is not more upscale than anything, but it's perfect.

Now, back to the cold drink problem. Dana ordered iced lemon tea and asked if we wanted some, too. Iris considers tea to be a weird-tasting thing grownups drink, but she heard the word "ice" and agreed.

Like milk tea, lemon tea is a homegrown HK tea concoction, served everywhere. I'm glad Dana introduced us to it, or I wouldn't have ordered it and wouldn't have known how to drink it if I had. The waiter set down four tall glasses of sweetened iced black tea. *With actual ice cubes in the glass.* Each glass contained three or four lemon slices, and Dana showed us how to use the long iced tea spoon to smash the lemon slices. "Hey, this tea is GOOD," said Iris, experiencing a moment of cognitive dissonance.

Dana later explained that one reason for the lack of cold water is Chinese medicine: cold drinks with meals are thought to inhibit healthy digestion. Another reason is that Hong Kong tap water was, in recent memory, unsafe to drink. It's now safe, but public opinion can't quite believe the good news.

This skepticism of tap water explains one of the most puzzling things you might see on your table at a Hong Kong restaurant: cups, plates, and bowls marinating in a brownish liquid. This is weak tea. The idea is to give patrons the opportunity to rinse their tableware with a sterile agent, just in case. (*The Sterile Agent* would be a good name for a spy thriller, right? You can have it.)

CHILD OCTOPUS

I worried that lemon tea might keep Iris up all night. And maybe it did, because I kept falling asleep (and waking up) long before Iris. One morning I awoke and was confused to find the living room curtain closed, even though I was sure I'd left it open. "Oh yeah, I got up last night and closed it," said Iris. "You were asleep." I'm generally immune to sentimental "my kid is all grown up" moments, but for some reason that was one.

Pitch and roll

Walk along Central Pier on Hong Kong Island, and you can follow a whim to any of the inhabited outlying islands. The tiny dot of Peng Chau island or the massive bronze Buddha on Lantau? Pier 6. Cheung Chau? Pier 5. Park Island? Pier 2. (This last one sounds especially scenic but is actually a massive housing development.)

Iris and I settled on pier 4, and caught the ferry to Lamma Island. The second-largest of the outlying islands (after Lantau), Lamma is a hippie haven. It's home to two small towns, Yung Shue Wan and Sok Kwu Wan. We picked the former, because its ferry was the next to depart. The boat was called the Sea Serene. The ride was anything but.

A ferry ride in Hong Kong rubs your face in a couple of facts about the city.

The first is that Hong Kong is a massive port. No matter which ferry you choose, you'll weave among container ships, tugboats, fishing boats, cruise ships, and occasional battleships. Over a thousand ships arrive at the port of Hong Kong *every day*. This is not news. "At the Victoria port he found a confused mass of ships of all nations: English,

French, American, and Dutch, men-of-war and trading vessels, Japanese and Chinese junks, sempas, tans, and flower-boats, which formed so many parterres," wrote one observer in 1873. (His name was Jules Verne.)

The wake of these fellow boats—many of which are larger than some of the outlying islands—presents a gut-churning obstacle course for a small ferry. Our boat pitched, then reared up and slapped its prow onto the water. "Are we sinking?" asked Iris.

"No," I replied, because I was fairly sure we weren't.

The second insight is that all of Hong Kong's islands are simply the exposed summits of undersea hills and mountains. We are interlopers on a wet planet. The ferry passed through the Sulphur Channel between Hong Kong Island and largely uninhabited Green Island, a forested thumb rising from the South China Sea. "What's that little island next to Green Island?" asked Iris.

I looked it up. "That's Little Green Island."

We swung around the western edge of Hong Kong Island, and Lamma came into view. The ferry docked at the north end of crescent-shaped Yung Shue Wan harbor, where a few fishing and pleasure boats were tied up here and there. The imposing smokestacks of the coal-fired Lamma Power Station rose to the south. To the east, we could just spot the rotors of a more benign power source, the Lamma Winds turbine.

Yung Shue Wan was once a fishing community. It's now a one-street town of gift shops, bars, and especially seafood restaurants. The leading industry of the Outlying Islands is luring people to their shores to sit by the water and eat fish. On the other side of Lamma, in the town of Sok Kwu Wan, the massive Rainbow Seafood Restaurant operates its own rainbow-painted ferries serving Kowloon- and Island-side. The ferry is nominally free, which should give you an idea of the restaurant's prices.

Back in Yung Shue Wan, Iris and I wandered past tank after tank of live seafood. "What ARE those things?" asked Iris, rushing over to a tank full of what looked like foot-long aquatic potato bugs. (Crayfish, I'm pretty sure.) This looked like a pretty good place to stop for lunch.

"Let me just check Openrice and make sure everybody doesn't hate this place," I said. I checked my phone. "Oh no, everybody hates this place."

Later, Iris explained to Laurie on the phone: "We saw this seafood restaurant that had all this crazy live stuff skittering around in their tanks. They were climbing over each other and were super active and there were a lot of them. But then Dada looked it up on Openrice. Turns out everybody hated it. 63 people said BLEAH."

So we kept walking. We explored the Family Trail, which cuts across the island, stopping at beaches and coves along the way, then retraced our steps and stopped off at a courtyard next to Yung Shue Wan's Tin Hau temple. Temples to Tin Hau, the sea goddess, protector of sailors and fisherfolk, are found all over Hong Kong, and after a typical Hong Kong ferry ride, it's not hard to understand why. Another temple lies just down the street from our apartment in Yau Ma Tei; it dates back to when our neighborhood was coastal, before land reclamation left it one thousand meters inland.

Iris climbed a tree and sat down to read a book. "I'm just going to stay in this tree until lunchtime," she said. And she did.

CHILD OCTOPUS

We stopped for lunch at **Andy's Seafood** and sat on the patio overlooking the harbor, eating salt and pepper squid and soy sauce shrimp. The shrimp were served with shells and heads on, but these were not peel-and-eat shrimp. If you haven't yet discovered the pleasure of eating shrimp whole, this would be a good place to pick it up. I don't see why it should be a controversial practice; who doesn't like a crispy coating with a chewy center? Close your eyes, bite into a shrimp head, and enjoy the fatty explosion of, well, better to just enjoy it and not think about it too hard.

A waterside meal like this isn't cheap. You're paying for the view, and you should watch out for upselling: ask about any menu item labeled "market price." But it's not outrageous, either. Iris and I loitered on Andy's patio for an hour, ate our fill of fresh seafood and rice, and got out for under $40.

Be regional

"A word of advice, my lad," he said. "So long as you are in Hong Kong, whenever someone offers you something to eat, accept it.... Besides," he went on, "Hong Kong is the best place in the world to eat. Promise?"
—Martin Booth

One night, Iris and I walked down Shanghai Street, past the plastic sex toy vendors. You know how sometimes you can communicate with your kid entirely with eyebrows? The nonverbal conversation went like this:

Iris (peering into a stall full of unmentionables): "Should I ask you about this?"
Me: "Not a chance."
Iris: "Okay then."

We walked underneath the expressway, and into **Woosung Temporary Cooked Food Hawker Centre**, a two-story building that seemed to be constructed entirely of tarps and corrugated steel panels.

Slapping the word "temporary" on a building makes the gods laugh. MIT's Building 20 was built as a temporary structure during World War II. Its inhabitants churned out Nobel-winning physics breakthroughs for the next fifty-five years.

A blog called Street Food (http://www.streetfood. com.au/2010/05/hong-kong-street-food-tour-day-1. html) visited Woosung Centre in 2010. "Next time we visit it will probably be a block of highrise apartments," the writers lamented. Four years later, the condos have yet to materialize. The place still looks like an oversized blanket fort decorated with colorful beer ads (San Miguel, great with stir-fried shrimp!).

Places like Woosung Centre exist because street food makes city officials nervous. Street food produces litter and unsolicited aromas; its hygiene standards are suspicious; itinerant vendors are harder to tax, and their restaurant neighbors complain; and street food has the whiff of poverty. (Do I need to mention that I love street food and I think these rationales are bogus?) For every city like the food-truck heaven of Portland, Oregon, there are a dozen Singapores. Like its fastidious neighbor, Hong Kong has spent decades corralling its street vendors into hawker centers. Few licensed stalls remain.

Woosung Centre opens early in the morning for congee and wonton noodles and stays open late for stir-fries and seafood. It contains several restaurants, all of which looked similar. Iris and I took a seat at a makeshift table and ordered from a picture menu: fried tofu with spiced salt and stir-fried beef with ginger and scallions. The kitchen at our place looked like it was hastily assembled from wares bought up the street at CCK, which it probably was.

The five-spice salt was excellent, and the beef was tender, and overall it was very much the Cantonese food I grew up eating in Oregon.

My favorite places to eat in Hong Kong, however, specialize in Chinese food from other regions. Great chefs from Sichuan, Hunan, Yunnan, Beijing, Shanghai, and the rest of China have all settled in Hong Kong. (So have great chefs from France, Spain, Italy, the U.S., Japan, and fifty other countries, but that's another story.)

San Xi Lou's signature dish is both delicious and hilarious. A Sichuanese restaurant in a high-rise not far from the Peak Tram lower terminus, San Xi Lou serves hot pot and a variety of spicy dishes (and a few mild ones). We asked for a small order of the chicken with hot chiles. When it arrived, I said, "I think this might be too much food." It was a Peak-sized mountain of dried red chiles on a shallow wicker basket. Hidden amongst the chiles were Sichuan peppercorns, bits of crispy bone-in chicken, and cashews. It's lunch and a scavenger hunt. Once you understand the gimmick, the dish is generous but not overwhelming, and the balance of spicy and floral and salty is perfect.

Sichuan peppercorns contain a compound called *san-shool* which makes your mouth go temporarily numb. There is no way to describe the effect of Sichuan peppercorns without making it sound like a trip to the dentist, but Sichuanese cooking prizes the combination called *ma la*, "hot and numbing": peppercorns combined with chiles. Most people who have tasted a *ma la* dish also prize this combination, because it's addictive. The day they invent *ma la* Cheetos, we're all doomed.

"I'm going to save these peppercorns for the end," said Iris. "That way, my mouth won't go numb and I can taste the rest of my lunch." Then she ate one anyway. Classic peppercorn junkie behavior.

Before the trip, Iris challenged me to eat a century egg. Also known, even more hyperbolically, as thousand-year-old eggs, century eggs are duck or chicken eggs preserved in an alkaline mixture that leaves the whites amber-colored and jellied, and the yolk smooth and gray. They're never cooked, just sliced and served with congee or chile oil or, here, with a mound of sautéed fresh green chiles.

Iris and I have traveled to Japan together, and she always warns me not to eat fugu, the potentially poisonous puffer fish. "Thousand-year-old eggs are like the fugu of Hong Kong," said Iris.

"So that means I don't have to try one?"

"No, they're just scary. You totally have to try one."

Well, the joke's on her. Century eggs are terrific, with or without a pile of peppers on top. The yolk, in particular, is as creamy as the best scrambled eggs. I ate a bunch of egg slices and sat back to collect my award.

"They looked too ordinary," said Iris, unimpressed. "I pictured them as more moldy."

From San Xi Lou, we crossed a pedestrian bridge into the **Hong Kong Botanical and Zoological Gardens**. Even though it was clearly labeled as such on the map, we were both surprised to come upon a row of aviaries, each stocked with a different menagerie of birds. We identified ibises, mynah birds, macaws, and pheasants, plus a owl strutting around sporting an outrageous white coiffure.

Rounding a corner, we passed between two enclosures full of cranes, stalking around looking fierce. (Wait, do birds even *have* facial expressions?)

Suddenly, all the cranes started squawking at each other. Iris and I dubbed this event "the crane freakout." Later, Iris called home and said to Laurie, "How much noise do you think it makes when a whole bunch of cranes are screaming at once? Well, it's a lot." We also peered into an enclosure containing what I thought was a tropical raccoon until Iris identified it as a ring-tailed lemur.

The reason we were walking through the Botanical Gardens at all is that I promised Iris we'd try a French chocolate cafe called **Jean-Paul Hévin Boutique et Bar à Chocolat**. The place turned out to be farther from our point of origin than I expected. We took a wrong turn onto an inhospitable road through the park and had to backtrack.

Let me turn this over to Iris, who wrote about our trip for a school assignment:

> We made it to the end of the garden and left. It opened on to a steep hill, so steep that the sidewalks had stairs in them! We walked down. And down. I was getting really hot. AND BORED.
>
> "Are we there yet?" I annoyed my dad. We reached the bottom of the hill and crossed the street. Then we kept walking.
>
> "Okay, we can turn here," my dad said. At least it was shady in the little street. Then we reached the end—and turned on to another street. ARRRGH.
>
> Luckily, we turned before the end of this street

(it was long). On the next avenue, we walked for a while. Finally, "Here it is!" my dad said. By that time, I was ready to stop anywhere.

The chocolate cafe was air-conditioned, and we ate a slice of cake and drank rich hot chocolate from porcelain cups. Then we headed back to our cruise ship.

We met up again with Dana Bruce for dinner at a Shanghainese chain called Crystal Jade. I've now used the term "chain" enough times that it deserves an explanation. You know your die-hard locavore friend who makes an exception for In-n-Out Burger, because the food is so good? Well, Asia is full of chains like that. Perhaps the best known is Din Tai Fung. When a Din Tai Fung opens in your town, you'll know it, because the line of people queuing up for soup dumplings will be visible from your living room window.

Crystal Jade is Din Tai Fung's competition, also specializing in soup dumplings and other fare from Shanghai. We planned to meet Dana there at 7 p.m. but got slightly lost, and then got sucked into Crystal Jade's byzantine take-a-ticket seating system, which makes perfect sense unless you're starving.

Dana opened the menu. "Iris, what would you like?"

"Soup dumplings," said Iris.

"What else?"

"Just soup dumplings."

I couldn't blame her. Soup dumplings are Iris's favorite food. Each one is a perfect slippery bundle of ground pork, kneaded together with gelatinized broth. The broth melts into soup as the dumplings steam. You cradle a dumpling in your spoon, nip a hole in the top, pour in optional black vinegar, and slurp out the elixir. Iris polished off two steamers full.

"Here's a question," said Dana. "If you could eat only one cuisine for the rest of your life, which would it be?"

"Asian," said Iris.

Dana and I agreed that this was cheating. She and Iris eventually agreed on Japanese. I slurped up some spicy noodles with pork and mushrooms, nibbled on seaweed salad, and took a bite of scallion pancake. "I'm sticking with Chinese."

When the walls came down

As I mentioned, Martin Booth's Kowloon of the 1950s is not so different from today's. The rickshaws are gone, the dai pai dong street food stalls mostly swept away into hawker centers.

The third notable absence is Kowloon Walled City. The Walled City was a former garrison, a few blocks square, that was excluded from the lease when Britain took over the New Territories in 1898. From that point, neither China nor Britain had much interesting in governing this postage-stamp-sized parcel of land, and it grew into a settlement so dense, it made the rest of Hong Kong look like suburban Wyoming.

The Walled City had a reputation for organized crime, opium, and prostitution. Booth, warned by his mother to stay away from the Walled City, made a beeline for the place and, if his story is to be believed, befriended a couple of Triad kingpins in an opium den. But the Walled City was also just a place where people lived and worked.

Lots of people. By the late 1980s, the Walled City was essentially built solid, an architectural parody of the surrounding city, fourteen-story buildings crammed together like a sleeping bag stuffed into its sack. Mong Kok, the neighborhood just north of Yau Ma Tei, is known as one of the world's densest, with 340,000 residents per square mile. The Walled City was *ten times as dense.*

The Walled City was torn down in 1992 and replaced with a park. Iris and I hopped on the MTR one morning and walked ten minutes through a quiet residential neighborhood to Kownloon Walled City Park. It is the opposite of its predecessor: tranquil, green, and dull, with a perfunctory exhibit, the ruin of the South Gate, and a small model of what used to be.

In a small way, Kowloon Walled City lives on in the book *City of Darkness,* by Ian Lambot and Greg Girard, who spent four years exploring, photographing, and meeting residents of the Walled City in the late 80s and early 90s. The book is long out of print and collectible, but will be published in a new edition in 2014. Its photos document a place that seems impossible but existed within recent memory.

I'm not sure what we expected to find at Walled City Park. Disappointed, we wandered over to the playground, cheered up by banyan trees along the way. Banyan trees are everywhere in Hong Kong; impressive specimens line the southern stretch of Nathan Road in Tsim Sha Tsui. Their adventitious roots grow in an above-ground nest, like the tree is going to scuttle around on spider legs, and the trunks remind me of how my dad used to entertain me by gritting his teeth to make ligaments pop in his neck.

It's a tree designed by the Ministry of Funny Walks. The playground was surrounded by banyans, threatening to become sentient at any time.

The City and The City

On our last night in Hong Kong, I had big plans. I wanted to go back up the peak and catch the billion-dollar skyline view, the one that looks like this:

Iris dutifully followed me onto the number 3 minibus and the Star Ferry. ("There should be a boat called the Pop Star," she said.) By the time we reached Island-side, though, she was ready to bail on my grand plan. Fine. So was I. We rode back across to Kowloon and watched animated creatures chase each other across the face of the International

Commerce Center.

"Why do I feel this way?" said Iris. "I should have said, 'Where's that bus? We're going to the Peak!'"

"Because we've been pushing it for seven days," I said, as we passed our favorite banyan tree, its roots illuminated at the corner of Salisbury and Canton roads. "Tomorrow, let's take it easy. We'll hang out at **Harbour City** and have lunch at Crystal Jade."

Harbour City is a gigantic shopping mall. It extends out into the sea on a cruise ship terminal at its south end and for blocks up Canton Road to the north. Near the center is CitySuper, a high-end supermarket whose various departments converge on a food court with stations devoted to Korean, Japanese, and Chinese food.

Wherever we went in Harbour City, we always passed the Laduree macaron shop. That's a lie. We never passed the Laduree shop; we always went in. I recommend the licorice macaron; Iris's favorite is the Colombian chocolate. Hong Kong is crazy for macarons, and they're even easier to find than egg tarts. Do they grow on banyan trees?

Before heading to the mall on our last day in town, however, we stopped at Kowloon Station and participated in an amazing feat of modern logistics.

Or, at least, our suitcase did. Both Kowloon and Hong Kong stations offer in-town check-in, where you can check in for your flight and relinquish your luggage, then spend the rest of the day baggage-free. We surrendered our suitcase at the Air Canada counter. It contained counterfeit and genuine Lego sets, Dark Chocolate Maltesers from Australia (like Whoppers, only better), five types of Japanese candy, a hand mirror Iris bought at the Temple Street Night Market, and a plastic whirligig toy from Kowloon Walled

CHILD OCTOPUS

City Park.

From the Airport Express train, we watched the Ngong Ping 360 aerial tram carry passengers to and from the golden Buddha on Lantau Island. Our flight left after sunset, and as we ascended to our cruising altitude, Hong Kong treated us to a final view of the skyline and the Peak, this time from 10,000 feet. We could clearly make out the IFC, including Iris's supervillain aerie.

Twelve hours later, in Vancouver, a U.S. Customs agent scanned our boarding pass, and an LCD display lit up. "Is this your bag?" she asked, indicating a photo of a black roll-aboard.

"That's it!" said Iris. I grinned, and suddenly realized what I had gotten wrong about the whole trip.

I'd imagined that Hong Kong would see me as a special person. Well, everyone wants to be the center of attention. Really, Iris and I were just two suitcases shuttling through a system that sees us, quite rightly, as cogs. The allegedly mature adult in our party didn't understand this at first, while the ten-year-old came to terms with it immediately: *they've got Legos and soup dumplings and the world's most beautiful skyline here; I'm good*. (The fact that Hong Kong doesn't stamp passports…we can agree that's bullshit, right?)

But that's not a reason to avoid Hong Kong. *It's a reason to visit Hong Kong.* The city is ready for you and the hundred thousand others like you arriving today. There's enough dim sum for everyone.

Our suitcase was waiting for us at the Seattle baggage claim, toys intact. I popped a Malteser and remembered our week in Hong Kong.

If you go

When you arrive in Hong Kong, you have two assignments:

1. Go to an information desk at the airport or an MTR station and a buy an Octopus card. It works on the Airport Express, MTR, ferries, Peak Tram, street trams, and buses. The MTR (subway) sells tourist products good for one to three days of unlimited rides, but I wouldn't bother: the Octopus card is so convenient, it's not worth the few bucks you'll save, and the MTR tourist passes only work on the train. If you have money left on your Octopus card, you can get a refund at the airport on the way home.

2. Stop at a convenience store (at the airport or any of the ten jillion 7-Elevens in town) and buy a tourist SIM card. This is a fantastic deal: 5GB of data, unlimited local calls and SMS, and even some credit for international calls and texts. It lasts eight days and costs about $12. There's also a five-day version for $9. At the risk of sounding like George

H. W. Bush getting excited about a supermarket scanner, having Google Maps in your pocket absolutely revolutionizes traveling in Asian cities, especially when you need to take a bus. While you're at the convenience store, buy a pack of tissues (to use as napkins).

Destinations

I've included links to Openrice.com wherever possible; on the site you'll find photos, reviews, and maps.

Andy's Seafood (http://www.openrice.com/english/restaurant/sr2.htm?shopid=3043&tc=sr1): Fresh waterside seafood on Lamma island. 43 Main Street, Yung Shue Wan, Lamma.

Chan Chi Kee cutlery (http://www.chanchikee.com/): A good place to buy CCK knives online is Chef Knives to Go (http://www.chefknivestogo.com/cck-cleavers.html). 316–318 Shanghai Street, Yau Ma Tei.

Crystal Jade (http://www.openrice.com/english/restaurant/sr2.htm?shopid=10639&tc=sr1): The food of Shanghai, including soup dumplings. Multiple locations including Shop 3328, 3rd floor, Gateway Arcade, Harbour City, 17 Canton Road, Tsim Sha Tsui.

Delicious Dumpling Shop (http://www.openrice.com/english/restaurant/sr2.htm?shopid=14613&tc=sr1) (美味餃子店): Exactly as it sounds. 88 Lai Chi Kok Road, Prince Edward

Du Lac Bleu (http://www.openrice.com/english/

restaurant/sr2.htm?shopid=2877&tc=sr1): Clay pot rice. 31 Jardine's Bazaar, Causeway Bay.

Emperor of Flavor/Delicious Catering (http://www.openrice.com/english/restaurant/sr2.htm?shopid=21617&tc=sr1): Great for breakfast, including French toast and milk tea. Multiple locations including 495A–497 Nathan Road, Yau Ma tei.

Famous Beef Brisket Noodles: Noodle soups including brisket, wonton, and fish dumplings. Corner of Temple Street and Hi Lung Lane, Yau Ma Tei.

Fu Kee Delicious Food: Tiny neighborhood dim sum joint. Just south of Famous Beef Brisket Noodles, Temple Street at Hi Lung Lane, Yau Ma Tei.

Fu Sing Shark Fin Seafood Restaurant (http://www.openrice.com/english/restaurant/sr2.htm?shopid=116272&tc=sr1): High-end dim sum. No, we didn't try the shark fin. Multiple locations including 1st floor, Grand Millennium Plaza, 181 Queen's Road Central, Sheung Wan.

Harbour City (http://www.harbourcity.com.hk/en/): A big-ass mall. 3–27 Canton Road, Tsim Sha Tsui.

Honeymoon Dessert (http://www.openrice.com/english/restaurant/sr2.htm?shopid=10576&tc=sr1): Very Asian desserts. Get your durian fix. Multiple locations including Western Market, 323 Des Voeux Road, Sheung Wan.

Hui Lau Shan (http://www.openrice.com/english/restaurant/sr2.htm?shopid=5566&tc=sr1): Fruit desserts, including great mango smoothies. Multiple locations including 263 Shanghai St, Yau Ma Tei.

Jean-Paul Hévin Boutique et Bar à Chocolat (http://www.openrice.com/english/restaurant/sr2.htm?shopid=82516&tc=sr1): Parisian-style cakes and hot chocolate. 13 Lyndhurst Terrace, Central.

King of Coconut (http://www.openrice.com/english/restaurant/sr1.htm?chain_id=10000220&chain_name=Coconut%20Milk%20%7C%20%E6%A4%B0%E6%B1%81%E5%A4%A7%E7%8E%8B%20(All%20Branches)&region=0&s=3): Coconut milk and sugarcane juice. Multiple locations including Dundas Square, 43H Dundas Street, Mong Kok.

Luk Yu Teahouse (http://www.openrice.com/english/restaurant/sr2.htm?shopid=1966&region=0&s=3): Old-school dim sum. 24 Stanley Street, Central.

Ming Kee Chicken Congee (http://www.openrice.com/english/restaurant/sr2.htm?shopid=11425&tc=sr1&con=phto) (明記雞雜粥): Roast meats, congee, and cheung fan rice noodle rolls. 1 Wing Sing Lane, Yau Ma Tei.

San Xi Lou (http://www.openrice.com/english/restaurant/sr2.htm?shopid=21564&region=0&s=3): Sichuanese cuisine. 7th floor, Coda Plaza, 51 Garden Road, Mid-Levels.

Tai Cheong (http://www.openrice.com/english/restaurant/sr2.htm?shopid=5522&tc=sr1): Famous for egg tarts. 35 Lyndhurst Terrace, Central.

Temple Street Night Market: Temple Street between Jordan Road and Man Ming Lane, Yau Ma Tei.

Bibliography

Booth, Martin. *Gweilo.* 2004. Also published under the title *Golden Boy,* this is among the best of many Hong Kong memoirs by British expatriates. Booth's adventures in 1950s Hong Kong are outrageous and thrilling, but the star of the book is his mother, who finds Hong Kong liberating in a way that could inspire an epic pop song.

Chen, Piera. *Lonely Planet Hong Kong.* 2012. The all-around guidebook to beat.

Connelly, Michael. *9 Dragons.* 2009. A silly but fun detective story set partly in Hong Kong. Detective Harry Bosch is not an adventurous eater.

Converse, PJ. *Subway Girl.* 2011. A charming young adult romance set mostly in Kowloon.

de Laurentiis, Giada. *Hong Kong! (Recipe for Adventure #3).* 2014. Did you know Food Network host Giada de Laurentiis wrote a series of children's travel books? They're not bad at all.

Dung Kai-Cheung. *Atlas: The Archaeology of an Imaginary City.* 2012. This is some heady intellectual stuff, a series of fictional accounts of the founding and history of Hong Kong as told by future cartographers. Clever and surprisingly hard to put down.

Hom, Ken. *Fragrant Harbor Taste.* 1989. Written before the handover, this cookbook is a useful guide to Hong Kong cuisine (I can't believe Iris and I never tasted fried milk!) and Hong Kong culture.

Knowles, Christopher. *A Week in Hong Kong.* 2013. The competition! Knowles knows a lot more about Hong Kong than I do, and he also makes Yau Ma Tei his home base. Forget I mentioned this delightful little book.

Lambot, Ian and Greg Girard. *City of Darkness: Life in Kowloon Walled City.* 1999. Out of print and rare, but a new edition is coming in 2014. *City of Darkness* is the illustrated story of Kowloon Walled City in the years leading up to its destruction. You will not believe what you're seeing.

Lanchester, John. *Fragrant Harbour.* 2003. A sweeping family epic in which several threads eventually come together in modern Hong Kong. Funny and beautifully written. Highly recommended.

Martin, Charles P. *Neon Panic.* 2011. A gripping detective story set among orchestra musicians in Hong Kong.

Mathews, Gordon. *Ghetto at the Center of the World: Chungking Mansons, Hong Kong.* 2011. Chungking Mansions, a building at the southern tip of Kowloon, has taken over from the Walled City as the place that visitors and locals love to swap scary stories about. Known as a den of iniquity, it's primarily a place where African and Asian businesspeople meet up to trade in all sorts of consumer goods. Also, it contains some good Indian restaurants. *9 Dragons* features a climactic scene set here.

Morris, Jan. *Hong Kong.* 1988. A highly readable history by a writer who has seen nearly the entire world and counts Hong Kong as among her very favorite corners.

Sasek, M. *This Is Hong Kong.* 1965. Reprint edition, 2007. One in a series of lovely children's picture books about cities of the world.

Shepherd, Bruce. *The Hong Kong Guide 1893.* Reprint edition, 1982. Many guides to Hong Kong for a British audiences were published in the 19th century. This one is notable for two reasons: it's available in a cheap reprint edition, and *it never once mentions Chinese food.*

Sterling, Richard. *Lonely Planet World Food: Hong Kong.* 2001. The restaurant recommendations are out of date, but worth reading as a general guide to the cuisine.

Acknowledgments

I thought this pamphlet of a book would be a small under-taking. But no book is small.

Thank you to Gary Lim and Fiona Cheng for stuffing us with dim sum, and to Dana Bruce and Wingyan Tam for introducing us to clay pot rice and Crystal Jade.

Jen Chiu, Becky Selengut, and Laurie Amster-Burton read the manuscript and patiently encouraged me to let my feelings out. I hate letting my feelings out. But they were right. Neil deMause read the manuscript on short notice, made some key last-minute suggestions, and never said anything about feelings.

CL Smith designed the cover and came up with the "Zip and Eat" name. Hire him at humblenations.com.

I hope Larry Adatto, DDS, will forgive me for saying "a trip to the dentist" like it's a bad thing.

Thank you to Iris, for being the best travel companion and kid, and to Laurie for encouraging our crazy ideas.

This book was produced with Jutoh (http://www.ju-toh.com/), a wonderful piece of software for creating eb-ooks. It's available for Mac, Windows, and Linux. The price is reasonable, and the creator, Julian Smart, answers all of my annoying technical questions. The first draft was, as always, written in Scrivener, the writer's best friend.

The photo of the Hong Kong skyline at night from Victoria Peak is by Nicolas Vollmer, licensed under Creative Commons CC-BY-2.0. See it big on Flickr (https://www.flickr.com/photos/nicolas_vollmer_photo/8610861172/).

About the Author(s)

Matthew Amster-Burton is the author of *Hungry Monkey: A Food-Loving Father's Quest to Raise an Adventurous Eater* and *Pretty Good Number One: An American Family Eats Tokyo*. He co-hosts the hit food and comedy podcast *Spilled Milk* (spilledmilkpodcast.com). Matthew has written for Gourmet, the Wall Street Journal, Mint.com, and the Seattle Times, and has been featured in the *Best Food Writing* anthology repeatedly.

Iris Amster-Burton lives in Seattle. She is willing to let her dad drag her along to Asia, because that's where the food is.

Made in the USA
Monee, IL
25 October 2020